COLOR

COLOR

a poem by Christina Rossetti

pictures by Mary Teichman

HarperCollins*Publishers*

Color
Text by Christina Rossetti
Illustrations copyright © 1992 by Mary Teichman
Printed in the U.S.A. All rights reserved.

Library of Congress Cataloging-in-Publication Data
Rossetti, Christina Georgina, 1830-1894.
  Color / by Christina Rossetti ; illustrated by Mary
Teichman.
        p.   cm.
  Summary: An introduction to colors and to poetry,
for very young children.
    ISBN 0-06-022626-9. — ISBN 0-06-022650-1 (lib. bdg.)
    1. Color—Juvenile poetry.   2. Children's poetry,
English.   [1. Color—Poetry.   2. English poetry.]
I. Teichman, Mary, ill.   II. Title.
PR5237.C6   1992   90-25588
821'.8—dc20   CIP
                                              AC

1 2 3 4 5 6 7 8 9 10
First Edition

The original illustrations were prepared as etchings created
on four copper plates using a color separation process
and printed by hand.

In memory of my dad, Raymond A. Teichman.

—MT

What is pink?

A rose is pink

by the fountain's brink.

What is red?

A poppy's red

in its barley bed.

What is blue?

The sky is blue

where the clouds float thro'.

What is white?

A swan is white

sailing in the light.

What is yellow?

Pears are yellow,

rich and ripe and mellow.

What is green?

The grass is green,

with small flowers between.

What is violet?

Clouds are violet

in the summer twilight.

What is orange?

Why, an orange, just an orange!

What is pink? a rose is pink
By the fountain's brink.
What is red? a poppy's red
In its barley bed.
What is blue? the sky is blue
Where the clouds float thro'
What is white? a swan is white
Sailing in the light.
What is yellow? pears are yellow,
Rich and ripe and mellow.
What is green? the grass is green,
With small flowers between.
What is violet? clouds are violet
In the summer twilight.
What is orange? why, an orange,
Just an orange!

About the poet

Christina Rossetti was born in London in 1830 and grew up amidst the rigid conventions and strict religious principles of Victorian England. She and her older brother Dante Gabriel, the famous Pre-Raphaelite painter, wrote poetry from an early age and were considered among the most outstanding poets of their time. "What is pink?," the poem from which this book is drawn, has been a favorite since it appeared in the volume SING-SONG, first published in 1871. Christina Rossetti died in 1894.

About the artist

Mary Teichman is a printmaker whose etchings have been exhibited internationally and whose work is part of the permanent collections of the Brooklyn Museum in Brooklyn, New York, and the Carnegie Institute in Pittsburgh, Pennsylvania. She and her husband currently live in Brooklyn, New York.